PENGUIN MODERN POETS 4
D76

DAVID HOLBROOK is well known as an author of books on the teaching of English. He was born in Norwich in 1923 and now lives in a village in Hertfordshire. He does some work with university students at Cambridge, but is now a self-supporting author. His works include *English for Maturity* (1961), *English for the Rejected* (1964), *The Secret Places* (1964), *The Exploring Word* (1967), *Children's Writing* (1967), *Flesh Wounds* (a novel), and a number of works of literary criticism, including *The Quest for Love* (1965). Of his three volumes of poetry, his most recent is *Object Relations* (1966). His five forthcoming books are on object-relations psychoanalytical theory, and the 'philosophical anthropology' of schools of thought influenced by Martin Buber, and the application of these to problems of education and culture. He has been married since 1949 and has four children.

CHRISTOPHER MIDDLETON was born in 1926. He has taught at the universities of Zurich and London, and at present teaches at the University of Texas at Austin. His volumes of poetry are *Torse 3, poems 1949–61* (1962), *Nonsequences/Selfpoems* (1965), and *Our Flowers and Nice Bones* (1969). His translations include Robert Walser's *The Walk and Other Stories* (1957), *Modern German Poetry 1910–60* (1962: with Michael Hamburger), *Poems of Günter Grass* (1969: in Penguin Modern European Poets; with Michael Hamburger), *Jakob von Gunten* (1969), and *Selected Letters of Friedrich Nietzsche* (1969). He edited the Penguin *German Writing Today* and wrote the libretto for Hans Vogt's comic opera, *Athenerkomodie* (*The Metropolitans*), which was first performed at Mannheim in 1964.

DAVID WEVILL is a Canadian poet who was born in Japan in 1935. He moved to Canada as a child and grew up in Ottawa. In 1954 he came to England to read English and history at Cambridge and, apart from two years teaching English at Mandalay University, he has made his home in England ever since. His two books of poems are *Birth of a Shark* (1964) and *A Christ of the Ice-Floes* (1966). He has recently completed a translation of the poems of the Hungarian poet Ferenc Juhasz, and he is now at the National Translation Centre at Austin, Texas, translating the poems of Janos Pilinsky. Both these translations are to be published in the Penguin Modern European Poets.

Penguin Modern Poets

4

DAVID HOLBROOK
CHRISTOPHER MIDDLETON
DAVID WEVILL

Penguin Books

Penguin Books Ltd, Harmondsworth, Middlesex, England
Penguin Books Australia Ltd, Ringwood, Victoria, Australia

—

This selection first published 1963
Reprinted 1965, 1969

—

Copyright © Penguin Books, 1963

—

Made and printed in Great Britain
by Cox & Wyman Ltd,
London, Reading and Fakenham
Set in Monotype Garamond

Cover Design by Peter Barrett

Contents

ACKNOWLEDGEMENTS

The poems in this selection are taken from the following books, to whose publishers acknowledgement is made: *Imaginings* (1961) and *Against the Cruel Frost* (1963), by David Holbrook, published by Putnam; *Torse 3* (1962), by Christopher Middleton, published by Longmans, Green. *A Group Anthology* (1963), published by Oxford University Press, had poems by David Wevill. The latter would also like to thank several editors who first printed or broadcast the remainder of the poems published here in book form for the first time, in particular Mr J. F. Kennedy of the *New Yorker*.

DAVID HOLBROOK

Fingers in the Door

(For Kate)

Careless for an instant I closed my child's fingers in the
    jamb. She
Held her breath, contorted the whole of her being,
    foetus-wise, against the
Burning fact of the pain. And for a moment
I wished myself dispersed in a hundred thousand pieces
Among the dead bright stars. The child's cry broke,
She clung to me, and it crowded in to me how she and
    I were
Light-years from any mutual help or comfort. For her
    I cast seed
Into her mother's womb; cells grew and launched itself
    as a being:
Nothing restores her to my being, or ours, even to the
    mother who within her
Carried and quickened, bore, and sobbed at her separa-
    tion, despite all my envy,
Nothing can restore. She, I, mother, sister, dwell
    dispersed among dead bright stars:
We are there in our hundred thousand pieces!

Reflections on a Book of Reproductions

Hours are a small thing, the interior
(Woman at tub, lamps, Vermeer's whore,
Onions or spinets) insignificant
At the time, in Time. But magnificent
The art's consideration of the body,
Nymph bathing; model, now long decayed,
Become Christ off the cross; the maid
Spurning the lover's flowers; old man
Blowing his smoke rings. And if I can
I would lay out the patterns of mine
Into something more than these nine
Hours since I woke this morning, one
For lifting a tree-stump, one to run
A Ford van round the shops for meat,
For onions, for fruit, and the rest we ate;
Another for a child's rest; another
For the two little girls to go to shop with their
    mother;
Then we all gather round for the tea,
All laying claim to her, or informing me,
Under the candles, about how they bought
A pair of shoes, and how the bus they caught
Struck the branches of trees, and what
The old man in the seat behind
Said to his wife, while they sneezed and grinned.
Yet this is the family food of the aspiration
To celebrate order: Bach's elation
Was nourished on soup and hearth,
And worked among insolent men; the bath
That bathed the *Badende Nymphe* was crock;
Snyders' lobsters were stolen by cats; the clock
Muttered rustily in their rooms; their studio fires

Went out; cursed their wives, imperfectly fed their
    desires;
And the artist would swear at his daughters who sit so
    prim
In the Kaiser-Friedrich-Museum, for ever looking at
    him
With tender and timorous eyes beneath simple crowns
    of flowers
A Dutch interior is but as clean and simple as ours.

So we are not demeaned by simplicity, or banality,
By our cars, electric kettles, or lamps; the finality
Of our death, even, in the mass-produced chest:
Burial may ennoble us, that we watch our best
From time to time put in the ground. From such roots
We may draw from the soaring elms, the yellow
Pillars of poplar, as each great red ball sinks below
Our pathetic horizon, some share of the significance
The great painters saw, between the small hours and the
    natural world's magnificence.

March Evening

I pace about the bricks with empty glasses,
Handfuls of papers, shovelfuls of ash,
Laying tomorrow's breakfast. So the evening passes.
I dust the telephone that draws its lash
Across my face at times, when someone's dead,
Hope's gone. Let no such bells shake motes tonight
We say; lock doors, rake fire, one light
Left for the children – then let's go to bed:
One more tired regular untroubled winter day.

And that's by inches how we edge away,
I think, and look out at the night. And there
The stars are signalling, three in a row. Bear?
Cross? A winking green, a frosty flame.
Hostile? Indifferent? Neither: calling my name –
Ten thousand marking out, not winter's bite,
But spring's warm blanket black: yes, cold tonight,
But green tomorrow. And so there I stood
Seeing the whole sky turn into Odsey Wood
Where we had walked that day, expecting March's
Flowers, but found December still. But for one small
  larch's
Dead wood spurting green, and then one more,
And then ten thousand, running across the floor,
Wood violets snagged by frost: and we're surrounded
By blazes we had missed on every tree, astounded
By what leaps out from each copse, equinox,
Caught out by fire from old sticks, bramble-stocks:
The stars, the woods, laugh at us as they roar
To their new perihelion, signal, semaphore
And win, before we've caught our April breath
Or changed our blood to suit. Preoccupied with death

I stood and saw the night's tongue flicker life's
Renewing; and as the black turned green, a wife's
Hand turned my head, she kissed my mouth,
And we began a new year's lease of growth.

A Walk by the River with My Daughter

(For Susan)

What did we see?
A horse, one cow, two cows, and a transformer,
The property of the Eastern Electricity Board,
Where, for a moment, holding the rusted paling
You felt the nervous hum of
DANGER.

That was what we saw.
Yet what I saw I could not tell you.
The matter was not that I could not count them
(As you thought I could)
The spikes of grass along the river wall,
Nor distinguish between Tufted Dog's Tail
And Rough-Stalked Meadow Grass,
Nor find the nest of the two birds that piped
Before the sun sank in the marshes:
Such the assured occupations of another age,
When the Plymouth Brother left his little boy with
    a notebook
Peering into the aquarium,
Or the Statesman warned little T.C.
Never to pick buds in the flower garden.
The Reverend Mr Crabbe would have told you
    what we saw,
In another fashion, on those saltings:
Your father can only see with difficulty
What there is here at all.

Not that my eyesight is bad, for when the Kingfisher
Darts from the sluice, I catch him in a corner

Of my vision, and you share him, and even now
Can I lead your rounded bright eye
To the fish flash as the grandfatherly heron
Bangs him on the water under The Rocks?

What did we see?
Remember we saw a transformer?
I cannot even explain the transformer
Except that it changes power into power,
And makes an endless exchange of energy
Which seems to me meaningless,
Much as the sun does, lying there where a King's
  Fleet
Once anchored,
Or as we do, even when we, like the fish in the bird's
  maw, we
Shall be changed in the twinkling of an eye:
DANGER
Is something I would not care to explain.

And as you grow older you will find your father still
  more evasive
On the subject of 'What did we see?'
You can countenance violence in the nursery –
The carving knife, the cracked crown,
'She whipped them all soundly
And sent them to bed,
And here comes a chopper to chop off your head!'
– I find it difficult: and do you see the give-away
As I wince, out of fear, and in shame?
And I am, I suppose, in a sense, irresponsible,
Seeing the sun fall like that in the marshes,
To clasp you to me for warmth as the salt mist rises.
I would hide the transformer from you under the
  grass

And hide the grass itself as it dies into straw on the
    dyke-wall,
Clap my hands to make the heron rise
And drop a wounded flounder in the water,
Restore, restore my heart again
By patching with pitch that rotten ribbed hulk in the
    mud,
Float it again, while you play in the bilge with a
    can,
And push off into the stream with the tap, tap, tap,
'That taps the tarry boat with gentle blow.'

We might pretend it was a victory
The seams might hold for a week or a month,
And what would we see?
The screws loosen in the rowlock sockets,
The ebb run and the flood flow,
Along each bank the high straw mat
Marking the long violence of winter:
Nothing spectacular, no redeemable flotsam,
But petty tidemarks of the world lining the coast.
And whether we went by sunrise or sunfall,
The one-legged bird beating up the little fish,
The mess of weed and jellyfish rising and sinking,
And behind us the oar-puddles spreading
Where I changed power into power.

But you, being young, would lose interest
Before one more day sank:
And I would lose courage
Before the October winds rose.
Shall we not go home now and share the same
    comfort
By asking each other:

What did we see?
And answering (for I can tell you that)
A horse, one cow, two cows, and a transformer,
Belonging to the Eastern Electricity Board –
Because this was written on it clearly enough,
And the word DANGER in fading red letters.

Apprehensions of Maturity

When it began, the grown man's apprehension,
Four or five years ago, I cannot place:
But I think it was not one woman's death
That set it off, though memory underneath
The scars of that falters, not wishing to see the face
Rigid over the bone, sealed in the final tension.

But even so, when I walk by my mother's corpse
Into the former rooms or under the poplar columns
That rose then as now, I find I was walking with
    death
Before his caprices with her: I foresaw the wreath
Laid on our familiar paths, the alarums
Foreshadowed as sundown declined familiar shapes,

And the large black barn drew the house and our
    square of grass
Into its ample oak-time; included us few sufferers
Among all the ones who had rubbed its lintels,
    merely
Passing from work to work, from web-dust to fresh
    starly
Nights, in the wind-cracked, under the sunstarted
    ferrous
Roof, to an apprehension of Time to which we
    belong, in which we pass.

Her death set the seal on that, for when the womb
In which one was softly formed, moulders,
The only escape from self-devouring immolation
Is compassion, an apprehension in another fashion,
Submission to the actual air, the underlying boulders.
No leap, no dig, no travelling can benefit the tomb

Towards which all must travel: only life
Can vindicate what's left in there for all,
And that's not much: under a shower of stones
We live, only surviving with the fortunate ones,
And exchange a little comfort while they fall.
When the apprehension took me I forgot my wife:

So of our ten years one passed in some numb
Separation by ghost, by haunt: and on her side
Haunted as much as I, but by an unseen
Affront to the springs of life. Between
The sun's uprising laid out across the tide
The morning after marriage, and now, where had we
    come?

Dragging each other down much, tumult-tired
As the children raved, or a work erected
Fell from its own, or the world's flaw, despite
Rainbow gleams against indigo, bright
Mornings then the apprehension, undetected,
Skulled both our faces, made our life undesired:

Desirable something elsewhere, Elysian,
Not with our own wisteria, kingcup wealth,
May with the applestorm, June with sun's affluence,
Or even with the morning fresh-fair to every sense,
Waterlights, tireless blackbirds, shingled surf,
    health
After sickness: even our love in the body derision.

And I contemplated Crabbe and his 'happiness
Was never granted', and the interloper's threat
Louring in Hardy's home: here was the bitter
Inevitable failure: cherish this, fault of better?

But knowing it sickening lie? Or had to forget
The shameful of dangerous rage, bewilderment of
   certain 'happenings'.

Thus never the joy in the morning street, fresh-
   showered;
Nor in the spring faltering down the shallies;
Nor in the orange stage-light on the elms after tea:
Darkened, twelve months, for me,
Despite what we sweated for, rallies,
And partial victories in sweetness, abhorred

Our marriage, our tongues together, ugliness
Stood in the room at night and spoke
Viciously, or retrospective there
Sowing division and sifting a gritty air.
I need not tell how this power was broke
By several life's works' skilfulness,

Not ours. Nor can I yet articulate the greater
Apprehensions needed for this, explain
What we came to explain, acceptances
Approached as shackle-roots, ending as dances
And undertakings undergone as pain
Growing to generosity and flowering sweeter.

Until this morning I noted with surprise
How much joy in an old peeling dead shrub-stem
Whitened by woodlice walks, or in the dull
Burnt honey-heads of clover, bruised rank cull
Of bindweed from the beds, hot phlegm
Of river mint and the great hosts of flies

That dally on the river, thickly breed
In heaps of lawn-mow, while the blue-
Backed swallows swallow them in strings
At speed in acrobatic flings:
Or walking in the street I remember you
Because of a lodging house's iron bed

I see in a window like the one we had
In Cornwall once, when we first slept away
Together. All that romance returns: the sea
Might be inland: I hear the gulls: yet we
Are many hours and miles from that today,
And many beds have known our births, our losses,
   and our dead.

Eros to Maidens

You will all of you have your quiet hours
Beside me in the meadow, in the church,
Even the playground, or among the flowers
Sent to your lover's grave: you see, the search
For me is out of Time, untouched by death:
Come with a sigh, I live beyond a breath.

I, Eros, Love, come when I'm least expected,
As I play Blind-man's-buff on crowded sands:
A boy will find my meaning in collected
Sea-fauna gathered by a girl-child's hands:
And there I sat, under the dog-rose bower
In Old Tom and his Anna's last long summer hour.

Sometimes you thought you saw me in a crowd,
Upon a bridge in Paris, keeping shop,
Or heard me in a courtyard sing aloud,
Or mounting your dark stair, made your heart stop;
But none of these was me: I passed by, blind,
My finger to my lips, leaving no print behind.

And in your single rooms sometimes you call
'O Love, please come and knock!' You mount the
    sill,
Go down to look for letters in the hall,
Or watch for him to cycle up the hill,
Or lose yourself at some wild party, gay,
But knowing all the time I am away:

And then by chance, some move of wrist,
Reaching for the same dish, or slant of sun,
Because his eyes were startled as he kissed,

Or darkness fell over you both at one
Break-barrier moment under the frosty stars –
You see me by you, know me as I pass.

Deepen that love! Secure it from the world,
For world within, without, will hunt to kill;
Time will assault, surprise attack, unfurled
Banners will sprout on every hostile hill,
And you yourselves can undermine the worst,
Betraying your own joys before their blossom-burst.

But, world and Time outwitted by my aid,
A thousand mornings sweeten what you have –
Intangible, a breath, yet growing made
Two bodies cherishing, become one brave
Togetherness, creating 'us', the life we've made,
A family, a home. Ah, these Time gave,

And Time and Death will take away;
But those who stay with me resign
To Time's dull turn, and yet are sure all day
Of how a constant love-light holds a sign,
Sunbeam on stone, or as colour in a flower,
That never moves nor blemishes, from hour to
     hour:

And kneeling by the pillar in the church,
Observing scratched-out names of the long dead,
The husband feels his wife's warm touch
Of arm and side; cold stone above his head,
Cold bones below, while candles hurt his eyes
And all that seems eternal is the courtesy

He pays to her and she to him in love,
From that first day she leaned across the fire
And moved so very slightly in her sleeve
He thought his heart would cry out with desire:
Desire their tenderness, their childbear, leave
   unquenched
As I revisit, live with them, entrenched.

You've not heard love talk thus I know before
Love has been falsified, made temporal,
Presented to your eyes as some blind whore,
Here for today, tomorrow damned to hell,
Untender, sensual. But now you know me, who'll
Simple, persistent, ask for not less than all.

From a Masque: *The Hedge of Flowers*

On an Overgrown Path

One summer's difference, between the clean
Spring spikes, the daffodils, and this
Choked October perplexity we begin
To tear from the bankside – withies
Tall as a child, willow, ash, sycamore;
The grass run everywhere we grope;
Nettle roots eaten into the barn floor
Between the bricks; the bindweed chains rope –
Wound over dry dead trunks; briars
Thick as a thumb and long as linen lines;
And woody nightshade berries' crimson fires
Hung in the dead espalier apple's ruins.
You and I stung ourselves and tore
This wild sun crop away from primroses,
Bared the black narcissus soil and swore
Next spring should pay in flowers for our bruises;
Wheeled away stacks of stuff to pipe in fires,
Or rot in a brown corner, chrysalis-filled,
Leaving the pool path looking much more like ours,
One summer's green sewn dragon's teeth well pulled.

But as we pause and kiss I look behind
And mark the path exposed, the damp sunk brick
I laid once, running over in my mind
What one had said, who never now will take
This path he loved again, who used to say
It looked as if it led to some enchanted lake.
Remembering this spring, too, when another lay
Dying, and here I fled the harrowing
Image of his unconscious hoar, in flowers.
I sadly break away and go back to my barrowing
To clear this nowhere-leading path of ours,

Many stings, spines and thorns away, and now
The dark tilth waits the frost, and here and there
I see a spike in place, buds formed, a few,
As their ideas survive them. Then a fair
Girl calls, grieving for her father still, and we
Offer what warmth we can, sharing the memory
Uncovered with the path that grows obscurity
Over itself, and pain and loss, as if deliberately.

Mother Nature, Mother Time

(On Therfield Heath)

There is a sterner creature in the brakes
And life with you, sweetheart, has grown so bland
I'm insulated from her, sometimes, her exigencies
   and aches;
Yet she sweeps round, in the October wind,

And cries out in the glow under the stripping tree,
Her hand clutching the branches as they grey and
   thin,
And when I walk the heavy dew, in front of me –
Her foot has bruised the high turf deep within.

I must go back to her, and her embrace
Alone on the pond bank where, brief, clear and cold,
She holds the sky's light over the one free place
In all the matted water, or flings up that gold

Tall afterbreath of sunset that fades with the dark.
Do not be jealous if I must belong
To this great woman ghost whose pictures lurk
In the sky's country, long scene, or the song

Given this late lit day, on a chalk hill
By one small lark, over the tall dead bents
That like a sparse white bristle overall
Clothe the high downs. And my three innocents

Dive in this grass pelt as I run for them
They disappear. I pause. And far away
The autumn slant light falls upon her hem
As she sweeps past, the bents bow to her way,

Cruel chill upon those children in the hill,
As though they'd never been, we'd never met,
I'd never middle-aged, nor yet grown fat,
No book-back faded; yet the lark sang still

With the old sound as when I used to lie
On warm wet turf like this, by such blue flowers,
Watching her stately presence in the sky,
Hearing her hoppers buzz, and smell her hay for
    hours.

Then thirty years passed as the breeze swept on,
The children leapt up, booed, and ran down hard;
She left us, and they, panting, fell again,
To watch pass by a thundering old Dad

Run like a boy, after his sometime Muse
Who now hurled in the beeches by the road and
    stirred
Bright mustard by a copse, leaf-lifting rose
To raise a migrant cloud that flew as one dark bird

Rather than thousands, and her bitter times
Return across that littered landscape. They run
    down.
We go to join you, their young mother, in the town,
And glowing from my chase I hear her toll the midday
    chimes.

Winter Sunday

So severe this black frost that it bent
The white burred burden of asparagus,
Hooped the old docks and broke the thistle's
    spent
Grey screws of spike and floss.

They lay rimed in their torment in each bed;
And as an epilogue
I heard a voice speak, and I turned my head
Only to see a leaf fall in the fog

Down the drained sycamore, like a withered
    hand,
Bough by bough, to the earth. No sound
But these few vacant yellow cackles, and
A dripping where the frost's grip was unwound.

The day went by expressionless and dead,
Winter-oppressed, and in the afternoon
We tasted his dark will, as foul and sad
The smoke-thick cloak came prematurely down.

Our boundaries unseen, the tree still speaks,
Dry word by ominous word,
Blackly of our decay: then the news breaks
Of a man in the fog, crashed dead upon the
    road

Not far from us. I go to fetch a child
Anxiously in the gloom: the streets are blank,
Only each chapel and the church are filled
With artificial light, where the hymns thank

Behind tall pointed windows, and the hot stove's
   steam
The only other lamps are in the butcher's shed
Where he kills for next day. And where a scream
Shakes the thick mist, where, in a breeder's yard,

Men urge a monstrous boar to mount a sow,
Their cold breath plumes, their raucous shout
Drowning the hymns, and the half-stifled low
Where the doomed cattle in the shambles wait.

Then the black damp falls suddenly, reveals
This winter grip as but a trick of light
To make us introvert: now as the great Belt wheels
Daughter and I return, breathe happily of night.

But I still taste old winter's intercourse of airs
That makes us swallow in the thing we are
Who breed and kill and feed and say our prayers
Against the cruel frost, against the voices of the
   sycamore.

Cardoness Castle

(Adm. 6d.; 10-4, Sun. from 2) a splendid 15th cent. tower (View)

The keeper stopped the mower on the lawn,
Pocketed a stray dead leaf, sixpence, and
Our compliments on his neat gardens, graciously,
And led us to the ramp. Here in a siege
They brought the horses in; here were the stores;
And once the sea came to the very motte.
Romantic, noble pile; we gazed and saw
Appropriate horsemen, rugged warriors,
Clan proud to war with clan, historic ghosts

But these too literary unrealities stayed there outside
Beneath the Ministry signs about the monument.

Inside we took a tour of human evil: here
Above the door a grating: small greedy brutes
Lured in their confidences, and then split their skulls
Or charred their guests' brains out with molten lead.
Step further: in the wall a privy, out
So that one ostler sat above another, jeering, near
An oubliette, where, dropped fifteen feet down,
Languished the captured enemy, oppressed, evicted –
With 'dangerous' ideas – and through the castle wall
A hole at which they dangled rich hot food
To taunt those dying, or extract by thirst
'Confessions', secrets names – and then destroyed
The turncoat wretches. From the vertiginous tower
Numbers had been thrown: before the stone fireplace
Dark wiry bloodsoaked men had writhed in pain
Whom no despairing linen-tearing lady there could
    save,

While from the slits shot arrows into trunks, while
Maid-servants cowered in sweaty rush-floored rooms,
And rats slid hungrily from enemy to tower
Where spilt blood, oatmeal, gunpowder and wine
Ran to the seadrains from the suffering cruel
Dangerous brown men, howling their uncouth
  tongue.

We came out in the sunlight where the grass
Shaved short, a harmless green, hid decayed pits and
  graves
Where lay those creatures' bones. And could pretend
Life was now orderly and neat, with flowers:
No daggers at our throats, no human herds
Unprivate closeted in exhausted keep alcoves.

Till we took up our morning newspaper
In the car, with the maps, again, and saw
THREE IN A PRISON CELL: on the same page,
  VICTIMS' HANDS
TROPHIES IN TRIBESMEN'S BELTS, and
  everywhere
More perfect treachery, without such weathered
  stones,
Protecting purlieus by poisoning the marrow in all
  bones.

Night Song

Stack the cups and clear away;
The bonfire sinks to ash;
Daytime is so much trash,
Night climbs the stairway.

We have done what we can to use the light,
Cricket and jar take over;
Children snore, the smell of clover
Tickles the poacher's nose as he treads it over.

Poppy and rose swim in the warm remainder,
Exhausted current of day;
Cold comes down from the air, hay
Hears warm in the field what the lovers say.

Bare to the teeming black the heady tree
Sighs in its sleep and stirs;
Softly an owl-wing whirrs,
The water chuckles, the paper beetle burrs.

Stack the cups and clear away,
The bonfire sinks to ash;
Daylight is so much trash,
Night climbs the stairway.

A Vision Dying

In the early morning, after another party,
I washed the many glasses with their lip-print
   marks,
But yours was not among them. There were moths –
A yellow swept-wing, spotted, on the ceiling;
A sweet brown, white-splashed creature on the sill.
Behind the pipes one struggled, large, but dying,
Its wings gone, eaten off, during the night,
Yet could not die, but fluttered in the debris,
I could not kill it mercifully, yet
Suffered to watch its stubbed chewed pointlessness
Quivering, vibrant still, in its web-littered place.

Like that your image dies. I dare not touch it.
I fight to kill you, chewing off your wings.
Yet when I come to find your broken body
I swallow meanings, as of indifferent things,
That lie in dust-holes, or between the stars.

We have no potency to alter those.

Convalescence

In bed a week, shrinks to the counterpane
The world, one's dealings, and the morning post
Lies next the medicine, torn envelopes – one's pen
Taken up now and then, idly, and then lost,
While you sleep, like a child, the books and other
    gear
Tumbling from the bed, an idle buzz-fly troubling
    the ear.

But then the racking ends, and the throat clears,
A fine day, and you dress, still tender, raw,
Invalid egocentric, and you go down stairs.
Still confined, you may cope. Until the garden door
Opens. Now there is more than overwhelm
Between one step and the next, huger than elm

Hail heaps of insurmountable: you'd forgot
What questions you elided in your daily course,
What unappeased jaws worked at you in every
    garden plot,
'Hold hard!' you cry. 'Don't press me!' But then,
    worse,
Counter-pane weak, neither escape nor face
You can, and stagger vanquished round your
    well-known place.

I walked so in my garden, cleared some sheds,
Lit a great bonfire of old wood and chairs; the flame,
Big as a woman, scorched the hedge and nettle-beds
In a great circle, orange-yellow. Then became
Cities on fire, death-camp corpse-burners, stake
Agonies, till my eyes and brain began to ache.

I fell upon my knees in the half-cut couch to pray
For all who died in fire, but my agnostic irony
Brought me back to my feet: what flesh-and-bone
    martyr
Could soar to heaven in that cruel tongue of fire?
I hoped that Joan died quietly, feeling my warmed
    cheek's pain:
Recalled the shouts of men in war who came to burn

In summer dusks like this. When the dead burn we
    breathe
Some of their bodies in our lungs, we fill our blood
With what they were who blow. The sap and varnish
    seethe,
A pile of papers climbs the flame, the black smuts
    upward scud.
What outlasts the consumptions of the world? Still
    whole again
I go back to live on, as the embers hiss in rain.

CHRISTOPHER MIDDLETON

Objects at Brampton Ash

The quick thrush cocks his head,
bunching his pectorals, halted.

Long holly shadows hone his shining claw;
you thumb its edge and grass gets grassier.

The tapered spire, at anchor in its ring
of tomb and cedar, has to quit ascending.

So you revolve in hearth-smoke's occult caves,
banished by touch of frost beading the roofs.

What increase, could these ends outlast
perpetual waste.

Seven Hunters

I

On skins we scaled the snow wall,
seven hunters; roped, leaning
into claws of wind; we climbed,
wisely, for no fixed point.
There was no point we knew.

Staggered upon it at noon.
Drifts half buried it. The coils
horns eyes had to be hacked free.
We lashed, as the moon rose,
its black flesh to sledges.

It was dead as a doornail,
thank God. Labouring
the way down, by luck
we found a hut, beer and bread.

2

Some came in cars, some barefoot,
some by air, some sprang from ships,
some tore in by local train,
some capered out of bed
and biked there with babies.

Like flies they filled the hot square.
The cordon, flung round that heap
of black tubes, when the eye blazed,
could not see. The crowd did.
Then we heard the first shout.

Now in our town the streets
and houses have gone.
Here, underground, we
who were seven are one.

China Shop Vigil

Useful these bowls may be;
what fatness makes the hollows glow,
their shadows bossed and plump.

Precisely there a wheel whirling backward
flattens them. Knuckles whiten on copper:
headless men are hammering drums.

Cup and teapot may be such comforters:
small jaws mincing chatter
over the bad blood between us once.

When baking began, the air in jugs frothed
for milk, or lupins. Now mob is crushed
by mob, what fatness but in wild places,

where some half dozen dusty mindful men
drinking from gourd or canvas huddle,
and can speak at last of the good rain.

At Porthcothan

A speck of dark at low tide on the tideline,
it could not be identified as any known thing,
until, as one approached, a neck was clear
(it is agreed that logs, or cans, are neckless),
and then a body, over which the neck stood
curved like a questionmark, emerged
as oval, and the whole shape was crouching
helpless in a small pool the sea had left.

The oval body, with green sheen as of pollen
shading off into the black plumage, and the neck
surmounted by the tiny wide-eyed head,
were not without beauty. The head was moving,
so like a cobra it seemed rash to offer
an introductory finger to the long hooked bill
stabbing the air. Danger had so
sharpened what intelligence the bird possessed,
it seemed to pierce the mind of the observer.
In fact we were afraid, yes afraid of each other.

Finally though I picked it up and took it
to a quiet side-bay where dogs were rarer.
Here the shag sat, happy in the sun,
perched on a slab of rock where a pool was,
in which I caught five fish for it
with a pocketknife, a handkerchief
and a plunging forefinger. But at six o'clock
it left the rock and waddled off seaward.

Though breakers came in high and curling
it straddled them, bouncing, buoyant,
borne along the sealine sideways, with head up,

slithering across the bay's whole width, and then
drifted ashore again, to scuttle flapping
with webbed feet flat like a Saturday banker's
to shelter on a level rock. Here it studied,
with the air of one of whom something is expected,
the turbulent Atlantic slowly rising.
What could I do but leave it meditating?

Early next morning, on the bay's north side,
I found it cuddled under the cliff. The tide
was low again. What hungry darkness
had driven so the dark young shag to shelter?
It did not resist when I picked it up.
Something had squeezed the cobra out of it.

I took it to a cave where the sun shone in,
then caught two fish. It opened one green eye,
and then another. But though I cut
the fish into portions, presenting these
to the bill's hooked tip, it only shook its head.
Noon came. The shag slept in the cave. At two
I hurried back. The shag was stone dead,
with its fine glossy head laid back a little
over the left shoulder, and a few flies
were pestering its throat and the fish scraps
now unlikely to get eaten.

                    Ten minutes perhaps
I sat there, then carried it up the cliff path
and across the headland to a neighbouring cove
where oystercatchers and hawks flew and far
far below in loose heaps small timber lay, tickled
by a thin finger of sea. There I flung the shag,
for in some such place, I thought,

such bodies best belong, far from bathers, among
the elements that compose and decompose them,
unconscious, strange to freedom, but perceptible
through narrow slits that score the skin of things.

Or perhaps (for I could not see the body falling)
a hand rose out of air and plucked the corpse
from its arc and took it, warm still,
to some safer place and concealed it there,
quite unobtrusively, but sure, but sure.

The Thousand Things

Dry vine leaves burn in an angle of the wall.
Dry vine leaves and a sheet of paper, overhung
by the green vine.
From an open grate in an angle of the wall
dry vine leaves and dead flies send smoke up
into the green vine where grape clusters go
ignored by lizards. Dry vine leaves
and a few dead flies on fire
and a Spanish toffee spat
into an angle of the wall
make a smell that calls to mind
the thousand things. Dead flies go,
paper curls and flares,
Spanish toffee sizzles and the smell
has soon gone over the wall.

A naked child jumps over the threshold,
waving a green spray of leaves of vine.

Climbing a Pebble

What did it mean (I ask myself), to climb a pebble.
From the head of a boy depends a very thin cloud.
A red speck shifting on the Roman Campagna.
This sea-rubbed pebble had no cleft for toes.

It is simple, the ant said (my Nares and Keats).
You start low down, with caution. You need not
slash your soles for lime like medieval Swiss.
No, but with spread arms, easing up, imperceptibly
colluding with the air's inverted avalanche.
This cushions, O, the aching spine.

A very thin cloud is falling from the sky.
A shot, a shifting robe of crimson,
whiffs of powder on the wind –
the sidelong buffet slams. And still you cling,
still easing upward; giant glades, they creaked and
    shone,
fresh mown, now small below – you do not smell
    them.

And you begin to know what it can mean,
climbing a pebble. The paradise bird
drops, dies with beak fixed in the ground.
An urchin made off with its cloudthin tail.
A cardinal, with footmen to load his fowling pieces,
peppers Italian larks a glass held spellbound.

The glass was tied to an owl, the owl to a stick.
I struck the pebble, digging, as the sun went up.

Edward Lear in February

Since last September I've been trying to describe
two moonstone hills,
and an ochre mountain, by candlelight, behind.
But a lizard has been sick into the ink.
A cat keeps clawing at me, you should see my face,
I'm too intent to dodge.

Out of the corner of my eye –
an old man (he's putting almonds into a bag)
stoops in sunlight, closer than the hills.
But all the time these bats flick at me
and plop, like foetuses, all over the blotting paper.
Someone began playing a gong outside, once.
I liked that, it helped; but in a flash
neighbours were pelting him with their slippers and
    things,
bits of coke and old railway timetables.

I have come unstuck in this cellar. Help.
Pacing up and down in my own shadow
has stopped me liking the weight it falls from.
That lizard looks like being sick again. The owls
have built a stinking nest on the Eighteenth Century.

So much for two moonstone hills,
ochre mountain, old man
cramming all those almonds into a bag.

Alba after Six Years

There was a winter
    dark fell by five
four noses ran
    and shouting children
she got so quickly in a rage.

Now when I wake
    through mist and petrol
birdsong cannonades
    blaze open-sighted
at a climbing sun.

Hopeful but prone
    I turn to face a wall
between me and that wall
    surprised to meet
wild arms which did not hold this way before.

Without Shoes

'. . . unbeschuht.' Mörike, *Peregrina*

One goes lightly
    down ignorant rays
across history buoyant
    with fruit and shade

One goes lightly
    mother and father wave
from dormer windows
    of the dove-starred house

Happy anthems –
    owls make naked
women laugh
    in the dark orchard

Babies chirping
    girls of cork
and moonboys quiver
    nailed by the bowstring

Perhaps an orange
    tastes of Padua
an alien chord
    spits visions

But one goes lightly
    over echo-dancing shores
up wrinkled lightning
    surges a friend

yielding tombs of air to trumpet wings
  along whose colonnade
without shoes
  one goes lightly.

Thinking of Hölderlin

(Hills near Heidelberg)

Never mind avarice; the hills
squander at least a sprawl
of steep oak. Speak
of the moroccan green
pines that fetlock them; of rumps,
rutted by axes; of bristling stung flanks,
flushed by puffs of cloud –

for first and last
who saw them crammed the air
with hawk and temple;
and what fetched them avarice, in the interim,
cannot change their green
bulk and butts of sandstone,
let alone rot the wits, killing,

as hawk and temple, his, for the crime
of being put, by them, wise to the least thing.
No, not in his name
do I join these crooked words, lest I miss
for him, more than temple, his hawk,
now lofted by their hot gusts, now
plucking the crowded vermin from their folds.

Five Psalms of Common Man

'Je n'aime pas le dimanche'

I

Whisky whipping g-string Jaguar megaton
sometimes a 'purely rational human being'

it's me they tell of yonder sea devoid of amber
it's me they tell of column and haunting song

noncommittal me my mumble eaten
by the explosions of clocks and winds without
   routine

not fountains not millennia of light inextinguishable
ebbing through column and throat with its
   wombwombwomb

come my pet my demagogue excruciate me watching
yonder fountain douse the yolky dunes

2

The creatures of coal have looked for you all over;
the creatures of tea heard a snatch of song, it was
   not you.

The creatures of smoke have looked for you all
   over;
the creatures of tar saw a tree, it was not you.

The hand was not you, nor the hairy ear;
the belly was not you, nor the anklebone.

The eyeball was not you. Tongue and teeth
and jawbone were not you. The creatures of hair

have looked for you all over; the creatures of snow
touched a locked door, it was not you.

The creatures of paper have looked for you all over;
the creatures of steel smelled thick wallets, it was
   not you.

These creatures wanted to be free to look for you;
and all the time you looked to be free of their want
   for you.

3

W. N. P. Barbellion (pseudonymous)
March 1915
sees 'on the top of an empty omnibus
a little heap of dirty used-up bus tickets
collected by chance in the corner'

felt sick
the number of persons
the number of miles
the number of buses

at all times
the number of voices
the number of voices not speaking to one another
perplexity without surprise

Avenues Madison Shaftesbury Opéra
the number of heart beats
without number

the sick one is he on whom his desire advances
   asking why

the sick one is he who has begun all over again
not waiting not
'waiting that hour which ripens to their doom'

he speaks (Adolf Eichmann April 1961)
'in starchy, clerkish language
full of abstractions
pedantry
euphemism'

4

My blind wife kicking in her flesh of flies.
My blind wife in her ring of ribs beating me flat.
But no shard of keg shall cool my last bones.

The flies were dancing in their ring.
Their ring was dancing in the flies.
The ring desired by the nature of flies.

Stomach eyes packing it all in tight.
Knotted wings kicking in a glue film.
Ghosted in glue was the nature of eyes.

Revolt severe if sieved for its ghost of motive.
Air without motive rubbing in the arid throat.
My blind wife I warm to the coolness of bones.

5

Order imagined against fear is not order.
Saith man. Fear imagined against order
only negates or does not negate existing order
Out of a rumbling of hollows an order is born
to negate another existing order of fear.

Nights broken before they end, interrupting
the millennia of my vigilance, saith man.
The nights of past time never slept to the end
re-enact themselves in the existing order of fear.

Another order of fear is chaos.
Images of chaos variously coordinated
by disparate imaginations accord or do not accord
to their seasons in time enacting the indeterminations.
The orders revolve in the ring or do not evolve.

The orders revolve as improvisations against fear,
changed images of chaos. Without fear, nothing.
Let me, saith man, take another look at the sea
    again.
And in his ear begin the rumblings of keels again.

The Child at the Piano

The child at the piano
plinking, planking, plonks.
I stare and stare. Twigs
angle the air with green outside.

Handfuls of notes, all happening at once,
her tunes do not occur; on their backs
round they whizz like stunned wasps; contour
would crush that kind of mass.

Telescoping flukes and faults, their
tenuous terrain dislocates
no spheres I know of. Her index rebounding
off high C beckons no hell boulder up.

The heroics, fatuous, ordain yet
this act's assumption of her whole element.
Boughs of sound swoop through the room,
happily, for her to swing from.

So I call my thought's bluff. My thumb
struts down the keys too, pings
to her plonks, on both white and black notes,
while the green air outside lets us be.

For a Junior School Poetry Book

The mothers are waiting in the yard.
Here come the children, fresh from school.
The mothers are wearing rumpled skirts.
What prim mouths, what wrinkly cheeks.
The children swirl through the air to them,
trailing satchels and a smell of chalk.

The children are waiting in the yard.
The mothers come stumbling out of school.
The children stare primly at them,
lace their shoes, pat their heads.
The mothers swirl through the air to cars.
The children crossly drive them home.

The mothers are coming.
The children are waiting.
The mothers had eyes that see
boiled eggs, wool, dung and bed.
The children have eyes that saw
owl and mountain and little mole.

Navajo Children, Canyon de Chelly, Arizona

You sprouted from sand,
running, stopping, running;
beyond you tall red
tons of rock rested
on the feathery tamarisk.

Torn jeans, T-shirts
lope and skip, toes drum
and you're coming
full tilt
for the lollipops,

hopefully
arrive, daren't
look, for our stares
(your noses dribble)
prove too rude

in your silence,
can't break, either,
your upturned
monkey faces into smiles.
It's no joke

as you grope
up, up
to the driver's door, take
them reverently, the
lollipops –

your smallest, too small,
waited three

paces back, shuffling,
then provided,
evidently

by a sister on tiptoe who
takes his hand, helps
unwrap the sugar totem.
And we are swept
on, bouncing,

look back,
seeing walls
dwarf you. But how
could you get any
more thin, small, far.

Mud-Dauber (Texas)

On yellow shanks which slot into black thighs,
hoisting his behind he crouches,
nose down, sipping mud.

Look long enough, if you can, to
measure the waist. The wings have spread,
or they fold up for poise.

Somewhere in that machine the grains
of mud get stored, once truly munched.
He licks the rock clean;

then bounces off, as if air were cushions,
hangs dazed, in mid-air, to spy out
some fresh crevice,

drops hard on it, and stoops again, quaking
in the static dive. His flight mimics
the buzzard's drift

along whatever warm current may offer,
over the barnyards and the airports,
creeks and turtle backs;

but is blinder, a black mist solidified
into the floating leggity tube
that lolls as it steers.

Then under eaves he mouths the pulp out
to the shape his trowel nose and hundred
voyages aimed at.

His colonies cluster; each nest shall hug
its dry egg by October; and the house
must wear that necklace,

while smoke of cedar scents our room,
and we lug by hand strong logs home
for the few cold days.

An Englishman in Texas

(For Donald Hall)

First he sees the sky. It is the one thing
not making as if to move. Far south
its blue excites the long spine
of hills. To fetch him
home from that higher tangle
could take years.

Coombs below those hills detain him. Sheep jaws
munch on berries which now ripen through
low thickets. A creek appears
whose yellow weed foam
ephemerids populate.
Limestone belts

polished by bursts of huge rain will occur,
across trails leading him from nowhere
to nowhere. The lizard gapes
beneath a boulder,
and admits, magenta-mouthed
the baked air

crusting some inveterate scarab. Twirl
of cardinal bird song and blue jay's
retch sculpt on space distincter
verges. Heat becomes
inhabitable, fresh-fanned
from their throats.

His haze diminishes, too, when one roof
of rusting tin has topped a hollow,

as if its apparition –
manhandled – had let
at last the estranged eye in
on something.

It hardly exists. Has stuck it out by
a mere stronger irrelevance than
the horned goat skull's candid gaze
levelled at his gaze
across curly miles of scrub.
Prickly pear

looks like a telling friend for time's cripple.
Dwarf cedars thronging undulations
balk grass and buckwheat between
those hills and his place;
so each dawn, like milk, they leave
his new wish

to be present, now, to drop character,
its greed for old presences, its dirt
fruiting demi-selves in groves.
Yet there still he prods
that suture of hill and sky
for ways through . . .

Help him, tall shades, Wallace and Westfall, whose
addresses, inconspicuously,
changed as men flocked round and round
your cockeyed cabins,
bleating and sad, agog at
the gun's wit.

Or do not help him. But let him move once,
free, of himself, into some few things.
Sky after all meets nothing.
And with my snake axe
I'll trudge to meet him, should he come
without you.

Itinerary for the Apparent Double

With you the lane winds uphill,
by day, hatching schemes;
by night, cockshut memory overhauls
your brooding mobile mind.

It steepens for you, on splay claws,
feeling the weight of eggs not engendered yet;
up the incline a lost day
floats its faint rose of shadows.

It is dark from the hill's foot to halfway up.
Boys with stones have smashed the bulbs; some
    shinned
corkscrewing up the posts, to rob them, furtively.
Morgue of maidenhead, *nigredo*, always foots the hill.

Here, for girls, black men come jumping
big from the ditch with naked choppers.
The mewing of owls armours them as they bolt
with goosepimples and their foretaste of moans on
    beds.

Yet with you the path can be picked out
from the furrow of hushed and curving space
dividing oak bough from oak bough on either side.
On the upturned face a breath of cloud and two
    stars.

All for you, who edge forward into the dark,
who have no mind to harp on foreterror,
trust these rounds of light, crossribbed by shade,
to be bodies, nameable, loafing against the fence.

Among them you mount the curve to the one lamp.
Here foliage hoards the spray of beams;
myriads of leaves have multiplied occult dawns.
So the beetle steals through moss in the summer
    night,

locked in his portable house, which he cannot enter,
and is overwhelmed by the cresting forests of
    chrysoprase.
You'd find it harder going, to their Cold Mountain;
always the snow cone with its ice flanks recedes,

brands in muscle the black joy of the primal
    motions –
mystery of effort, this seeming barely to move,
till the body, twice-born, swells with tender power,
raging afresh to expel the last stride.

It might be something, to have lived like this,
with a vacant air, behind those blessèd eggs.
Yet you crossed the ridge. You have begun to drop,
free, from the zone of calm that is gorged with
    nothing.

Or does another day convict by the death of so
    many,
the slope sucking you under as you run to the
    choked town
through shrieks of birds that flash in the sun like
    axes.
What pain you have to bring, from ignorance,
    always.

You flail the earth with it, you track the sun's wheel,
either way, up or down, following everywhere the hill;
the child of ashes has it for a spoon;
it domed the round Iberian tomb before Carthage
  came.

So you are continuous, and might have been noble;
but you will forget and I forget what you have
  forgotten:
how deep the hill shines under its shade of tall
  trees,
and when no stars come, goes to them darkly
  upward.

Octobers

They watch the big vats bubbling over.
They walk forward, fists dig
into hip bags and sweep in silver arcs
the seed. They put ready
files that will rush from room
to room when the crisis breaks.

They rake the pear leaves into piles
on lawns. Among square mounds
of air bricks they prepare foundations.
They return, with faint tans, to renew
their season tickets. They are giving
again the first of last year's lectures.

They remember Spring. It is the walk
of a woman otherwise quite forgotten.
Wondering if it is for the last time,
they drive through the red forests.
They control the conference tables
with promises of mutual destruction.

They put the cat out with unusual caution.
They clean the flues. They fall
flat on their tough backs off mustangs.
They visit the rice and the apple barns.
They man the devices with fresh crews.
They like the o in the middle of the name.

Amour Fou

The hand taking the hand holds
nothing. And look. The trouble
with two sets of eyes
is that each wants out.

Islands. But we float; if face
to face we sit down in bars,
our space acquires us,
orphans of blue dust.

There is a call for help, milking
an older silence than can give suck.
Me, I shall not resist.
An owl should adore the empty air.

So make your body from the heap
of shadows down my mind. Nothing's there
for you to resist. Today, dear house,
you've not a thing that's mine.

Mirrors – not needed, we
are detached otherwise.
Chairs and shoes, our
dependants – gone.

To the call, the one perplexed
voice, calling, replied
less and less. Darkening our room,
these are the mountains we roll.

Old Bottles

It must have been long
I lay awake,
listening to the shouts
of children in the wood.
It was no trouble, to be awake;
not to know
if that was what I was.

But I had to buy
old bottles, barter
for steerage, candles too,
each stamped with my name.
It was hurry hurry
racing the factory canal toward
the town of the kangaroo.

Up the street I came
across a knot of dead boys.
In the room with a flying bird
on practising my notes
I found its lingo;
my body knew
those torsions of the cat.

She came by, that girl,
she said it's to you, to you
I tell what they are doing
in South Greece and Germany.
My parents killed, brother gone,
they read this letter, I'll
not be here, you do not understand.

In my striped pyjamas
I was not dressed for the journey.
I changed into padded zip
jacket, boots, canvas trousers,
my pockets bulged with the bottles,
I was carrying the candles,
and I ran and I ran.

DAVID WEVILL

The Two-Coloured Eagle

The last days wrenched her inward completely.
Her beak scraped inner brain,
Her skull turned to old rocks and the wine seeped
    out dry.

Under her hooded scrutiny now
The Rhine flows on, without help; she can't stop it.
In the perfect dead breathless quiet
Her only sound is the blind deep drumming of barges
Tugging her weight, tapping
Northwards, against the current.

Snow must fall like bone-meal here,
And success fledges no new eagles. We paw
In the cold, towards her warm red side
Of sunset, where the aching black
Grapes shiver their tinsel warnings at birds.
On either side her wings are folded, hard.
Her back is against the south,
Her brackish beak is raised to the North Sea.

Now her iron-age furnace heart
Hardens too, with October, the dead in our bones.
It is a grim place to bring love.

Snow

In the painkilling cold that wrapped
A frozen skin of trousers round his shins,
His ankles in irons, eyelids locked on the air
Barely watching the branches of pines and wind
    gathering
In shifts, snow-socketed and numb as needles,
The sun a pale distraction but never the heart
Of his ice-feast; walking the car-tracks
Woven and crossed like firehoses along
The hospital road, walking, or rather sidling
Frontwards, and thinking, 'Here's this vast white
Revolution, I alone am carrying sex
In our world, something precocious which the sun
Notices moving, of its own will, outwards,
Blemished by motion and by its own unique
Dirt-carrying will, intelligence of squeezed eyes
Against the disembodying white of the land –
Something that parcels the world by walking out
    here
Under an inch of wool, upon rubber feet,
Defying nothing, but touching the limits of cold
Humourless as a locked brook
Or an icicle.' 'I am not alone because I bring
One thread of life into this weave of death,
And each is as whole as the other: sex is warm
In my coat but cold in my shadow, sex
Is broken in the pines and in the bland birch-trees,
The permafrost, of which I am no part,
The rock-hard doormat of grass underneath, the
Scrapping chickadees on the dotted snow, –

All tension, teeth! I alone am above it, indifferent,
Bestriding this difficult time, watching
A world where everything comes out right if
Left to its own cold course: I, knowing my tracks
Will turn later to meet it, its death unsolved.'

In Love

She touches me. Her fingers nibble gently.
The whole street leans closer, its doors
Grin open and cluster shut,
Gathering like a first closing, firmly.
Warm Sunday mornings breathe a way of knowing
God's love, his shuddering mouth to mouth
Vision above the brain's heat,
Beyond leather foot, bible, or prayer book –
Naked, we push their webbed stares out.

Look, bodies that puzzled me no longer love;
Effulgence of grasses cover her body –
I champ and am at sea and drown and feed,
Hurl and kiss, climb and descend,
Lie still with the prickle of ants underneath me.
There was an opening, an opening –
It's gone now. Now there's no question of fire,
Grasses, or drowning; only this first
Dry building of rib above rib, as if
A great house crumbled on its skeleton.

And this is my Sunday lesson she teaches me.
Her texts are pillows, strong wrists and liquid
    ankles.
I could paint her as I fell on her,
And did, with my tongue, lungs and my whole heart,
Each breath exploding its hot ether lash
Through our wills to their blind core.
If this is love I grieve for God's
His idolaters shuffling by with their scrubbed
    children;
Though her face, with its sky-change coloured eyes,
Melts them all one in my privilege.

Street Stroller

Striding too slowly to catch up with that glint of
    sun
Which might have held a Chinaman, a cat, or a
    butcher's
Work on a missing body, I know
Health comes with facing horror. I find
Dreams flesh me so closely my muscles become
    poisoned,
My body fitfully weak as the scene of a murder,
A disappearance, or an unknown animal . . .

Struck dead, this city's pavement spits out rain,
Unfamiliar as New York, or Phoenix. My bedsheets
No laundry would accept now, knowing my sleep –
Such unrest has no specific outside itself.
I have created my city in a minute's open hand.
Its eczema spreads, to infect my whole body.

My Father Sleeps

Who brought from the snow-wrecked
Hulk of winter his salvaged
Purpose; who came, blind but friendly
By these lines his mouth and his eyes
Have fixed; and without further talk
Taught me at last how to walk,
Until by his power I came
Out of innocence like the worm's flame
Into daylight. What practical need
His patience had, and anger bred
Of disillusionment, has gone with age,
I have this white-haired image,
Arrogant perhaps, and too much the hero
For our friendship's good: Lear, although
Afraid of words as of madness,
Of procrastination as of disease –
A lover of plain-spokenness –
Though not where it hurt, that he could understand.
If I trace the scars in my right hand
They tell me of purpose disobeyed,
Of old and factual truths my head
Cannot alter. And watching him thus
Sprawled like a crooked frame of clothes
In the sleep of sixty years, jaws firm,
Breathing through the obstacle of his nose
A stubborn air that is truth for him,
I confront my plainest self. And feel
In the slow hardening of my bones, a questioning
Depth that his pride could never reveal;
That in his sleep stirs its cruel beginning.

Spiders

Muddling up the wooden stairs one night, in my
    socks
Past screens and shuttered bunting-creviced
    wallboards,
My tongue dry, but a cool wind puffing thinly soft
Up my torn shirt-front, the dust hot-thick in my
    hair,
I crossed my sister coming that way in her slip –
The steep way down, half-asleep; her chicken-hearted
    breathing
And toes antennaed for spiders or bits of fluff
That might jiggle and spill a mouse. I tasted my own
    breath
Kekking, milkweed-sour, after the beer –
But not to budge, or her shriek might wake the
    house –
Who is it ! I didn't know her face –
Such full pails for eyes; she might have been glass;
The roman nose, pink lips peeled white over salt
While ten years woke up and started . . . I thought
    myself
Back, a loiterer in jeans, hands spittled with oil
From throbbing handlebars. Wind shoulders the
    porch,
Flickers the close trees. . . . I held back then
And jammed my buttocks hard against black wood,
My back a prickly heat of rusty nails which
Builders'd slapped in, and left, when the lake was
    young
With all her forests open to the wind, mated
    conifers
Exploding dry cones. I listened in the dark,

And thought, this wife won't wait to be woken by
   me,
But go on down, passing me, always on my left –
Wind clacking the picture-frames through our big
   house –
I wasn't going to wake her. I mightn't have seemed
Her brother, then, but eight legs sprung on her
   dream,
Something she'd sense far worse than spiders, on
   the stair,
That could harm her children. Maybe it wasn't just
   fear,
Or concern, that made me cringe from her.
Two people who cross in the dark walk nearest to
   ghosts,
Her terror might have stuck its mouth in me,
And sealed her against a love she could not cope
   with,
Grinning under heavy sheets, with her heartbeat.

Boy with Cancer

The days stood still, and he looked and saw curtains
Light as cirrus, and a blank window unframed.
A whine of leaves came to him, from the summer
Beyond, from the wind sweeping loose hair of days
Across the frontal wall, across the eyes
That kept a world in store.

Thinking, what is a lean stick like myself
But a switch to knock flies off fruit in bowls.
A knife to scour the nitre from old walls
Where rot is endemic,
And the encrustation falls, each day by day,

And mornings hesitate. . . .

Realize, he said, the time is come for action;
Divide this, and this, and quarter that
And the sun must be a newer, clearer vision.

And the sun will be as a sky, with wheeling clouds,
Snowflurries above high summer.

But the days slumbered, and the sun stroked
Every hour as it passed the finespun curtain;
And the whine of leaves grew to a buzz of flies,
The hidden wall crumbled, his head
Sank like a stone into his palms –

All around, the noises, the noises
Fell still.

The Conscience of Gardens

Earthworm was crushed by a shoe,
Quirk stiffened to this varnished shoelace
The cat's nose rasps over, pinched for a smell.
In our garden the apples were all taken by boys,
A few plopped and broke, made
Rubbery pies where the brown stains bored
Entering them. Standing at the kitchen sink,
From that window downhill, the squared grass heaved
Thick with crumbles of soil. I remembered a boy
Three days before Bar Mitzvah, drowning there
In a deep drift one winter, though that garden was
In Toronto, and I'd read it in some paper.
Still, disasters only happen in one garden –
Ours; that dappled mapping of hedge
Where wolves run, and the moans of a wife flayed
To a cinder by paraffin and a jealous husband.
But that was farther north, in a forest shack;
Though the witnessing trees were those dwarf elms
   there
Which we pruned with shears each spring, in whose
   shade
I crammed Latin for tests that never came.
We hate our garden. It is full of the odours of
   growth,
Worm-seeled, and sparrow-dabbled,
With hints behind each moss-pierced shed-board,
Each stray and legless rake and molared shovel,
Of rages healed by other people's deaths
Not of the family, but in our heads, still;
Who were good neighbours above my skilless pride,

And would never murder, though one shotgunned his
   guilt,
Eyes humbling imagination, his children gone,
While our garden thrives, and its apples snap their
   cords.

The Poets

A hard coming we had of it
Everybody influencing everyone else
And the critics chafing, rude, disorderly
Cold on our tracks. No sign came
Proving winter was summer. The drab snows
Choked, spent, and left
Our deciduous gardens rusted black as bolts.
Though some found fame. The individual Christ
Slow to appear as ever, was hustled in
Drabbed in a busker's coat and sailor-pants,
Coy behind spectacles. We watched him. Some sat
Listening at his teeth, the rest
Gave orders that he should be buried lest
His bite prove deadly. But under it all
Was the shaping edge of our wisdom that
Disowned such praise as he gave. He died.
And summer came. The critics sat
Sleek-feathered on the shuttered hills
Gnawing a rat's backbone. We decided
The omens were bad that year, and squatted, numb,
Bunched over our fires, bled the land hard.
If it were not such effort to start again
We could continue our journey on to the cold,
And build our crude villages under the frown
Of friendlier hills, where the vultures eat vegetables.

Last Settlers

Whoever lived in this house commanded the valley,
Hawk-wheel and crow-glide, all his. Ten miles
From heel to lip and steep-ravined,
Farming made hard by nettle-spike and rains;
Slope-shouldered, bow-legged men, mules, lanterns –

He planted tea. But nowhere in the scrub
Boulder or rock-fall water, now, do his whims
Outlast the jungle. Machines
Litter and rust the dry yard; her womanly cannas
Nick the blown grey valley to uncertain crimson –

Huddle like bathers. Behind its locked
Windows the house will age; worms
Freckle the weatherboard with statements, words
Phrasing their dumb tenancy, stunned
Like these veering kites that soar and press
To a tremble at the roofed hill's lip –

No settling there safe enough yet to evade
The militant dog-print on the lawn, or rash
Quipping of parrots, emerald-backed
And canna-crested; who mock that couple-voiced
Going from these heights, these pounding shores of
  wind.

The Pilgrimage of a Wise Buddhist

Self unmeriting, receive my gift,
The parcelled herb a fruit of sorts
In season; but plucked from a poor tree.
An age had gone before this thorn

Filled to flesh on the branch (which housed
A wooden horse and rider, chipped
And knocked as if needing the gift themselves).
This is my first promise –

Not a leaf more than I can afford,
In season or out of season:
For my wife and her one daughter
Obedience, and a fire to spread

Hands for my homecoming.
For my dog and cat a bite
Of good flesh (not mine or my neighbour's);
An affluent portion of rice, quite enough.

No more of this herb. Try
The star-flower, leeked in white
White and red speckled, like a pox;
That this hand in the till of my shop

Keep true account against thieves;
That my sons come of age to meet my age;
That my woman's hands be full to the pride of my
    touch;
The jungle reply twice to my gun.

And may this bowl be dung in the hand
Of a thief. And I, merit the beggar's
Greed of birth if I should own
One bullock above my neighbour's need.

Next month I will come with two bowls.

Monsoon

A snake emptied itself into the grass.
A lizard wriggled out of a cup of ferns.
The pebbles, quiet, but nudging to follow the dust
Downwind, struggled with consciences,
Vaulting back as the gust, passing, kinked the long
    grass.
Then first we heard it, the long rush and rake
Abrading, stripping the earth's back, as the rain
Trailing its millions of wires, and voiding first
The lecture hall, the library and bungalows –
All the gardens springing taut, and the tennis courts
Smudged like wrecks at sea – the downpour came,
Caving its seething wall onto our verandahs,
Submerging the whole house. And we froze,
Like water-spiders clenched in their sacs of breathing,
Crouched, dry and firm in the damp close mouth of
    the wind,
As the tropics snapped and tore at our moderate
    blood –

Then after an hour the ground steamed openly.
The rain, flickering northwards into the shallow hills
Left little puddles behind, rubies aflame
In the fattened grasses drinking the sunset down,
Deep, through stem and root, and into the cave of
    stone
Where the scorpion hungers, carrying his bruise down.

Swans: Nottingham

Swans clap and skid their hatred across
The pond. Whose swan is an albatross
Braves traffic to avoid the clapper beak,
Or throws stones, to watch their feathers shake
For cover, out of spite. They too go grey
From feathertip to eye, and legs drag
Down roadways cross-water and suddenly –
Your conscience bowed at the pool's edge –
Pull free this spongy bulk lassoed to weed,
And wish your stones had killed before this one died.

Sometimes I startle in your face
The Grimm-child returned to swans; that grace
Of monster's neck swung deep to bite
A brush of tail between their lazing paddles. At
    night
Tucked down a shoulder of the cold lake,
Their cleft wings buffet your sleep. But stones
Your hands have picked are harmless; my stones
Raking the pond's edge want heads to break.

Flying Fish

Swims with the long swirl of eels at first; then
The sharp quick wake, a white scar breaking
Across the wave's side like a cast line. Instinct
Confuses ship's wake with wave, imagining
Rearing walls and valleys past which escape
Teases the knifing fins to wing

From wave-ridge to ridge. The world swims
Through this fish, swells, bursts over his eye
In cold fevers; subsides. Whole schools may
Scatter away on a fin, leap-frogging the spray
The ship's dead iron plunge throws back like hair.
Sometimes they wait just under a wavehead; lie

Still and patient as bait, peeldrift; then suddenly
Across a warm magenta sea the silent
Scream of their flight drums on a wave
That baffles them, feels solid, drives them spent
Downward, or spits them up like rain-beats
Off a pavement. By no accident

Will these fish climb to poison the sea's calm
Defying the bitter-as-salt air they may dive
Briefly, upward, like Icarus to waylay
The meridian sun; or they may strive
To outplay some vair-edged shadow that startles them
Fathoms beneath: and swim through air to live.

Immodest Bullrush

My hands burn yellow on her stalk.
Her head is fully six feet high
But reduced by winds to a clattering pole
Like corn, or sugar-cane. Of these ones
Strapping the pond's edge none is taller, more
Gross, with her packed head's bulk, as the sun
Seeps through her brandished welt of husk, up
Like a glare off the water to drench
Appraisal. Electrically it grips –
Her dragging stem. And the will it obeys
Is the one will of her discoverer to whom
Touching is not enough, and having is all.

Rubberneck

I'd like to be solid as this pebble
So motionless and tense I could crush the air
Out through my pores, and be numb
To the difficulties of being sociable.
Now, as it happens, I take my air
Like a trembling leaf, and need it.
My forehead's struck with a festering rash
That the merest of choices must aggravate –
Like a wheat rust. My neck is a gale,
My hands sweat like tongues. If you knew
What shrewd competence sits in my glance
What furious bespectacled critics come
Running from my hair shaking their stiletto
Pencils! – as if to scratch at lice –
You'd pray aloud to your helpless devils.

Though now as my head swivels constantly
I see everything plainly because I know
Nothing once, but it must be confirmed
By this perpetual reappraisal. And yet
The roots of my eyes resist. I am blind, I think.
I am chance itself and the missing link.
To have my crust I must eat it. In me
All time has its place but nothing survives.

The Venturers

I pull the blankets close, so she'll keep warm;
Their soft bulk sliding off like unroofed snow
Woke me from my dream: a quarrel of pigeons
Collapsing off the eaves, clattered into the night
And to what high homing under the eagle stars
And avalanche, flapped across the Milky Way;
Their wings luff with the curtains, my bloodbeat.

Their going's not worth regret I think, lying here;
To nest on the hilltops, muscling up supplies,
The air's skate and stumble, up the most difficult track
To the hearth and mouth. But tempers break
With the animal back; the bull's pizzle and the thorns
Can goad me only higher, beyond all goals;
And the hobble and jess of her hand on me
Cannot be let go, or lost. The dark chimes four

From a neighbour's clock. Crunch of the first tyres
On the ice-rutted snow, the waking birds, will begin;
And others, rending beyond their lit eyelids will
Bury the beaks behind, the squirrel's shrill claws
That twitch my hand against her sleeping side.
And fires will knot the clockhands to hard worms,
Our earth's focus still: my crouched two eyes
Staring into the dark that is dark within;
And hers locked shut on a sleep where daylight spins
Words in the dream-kept head, bright stolen world.

Body of a Rook

God broke upon this upturned field; trees
Wedged tangled and thick as black crotch-hair –
But an eyelid in the field's face flutters,
Winks, blindingly. Whose
Sunrise through that blazing shrub glows
Ram's horns? twin forks of a tree,
Dividing, splitting. And nothing disturbs
These soft tussocks, the woman's one-eyed love.

In the scenery of crushed glass, here,
Among kneading hands of mud, the scoured head
    lies,
A world seized between sunlit clouds,
Spinning with sense, one eye gone black.
I stare out over my roof of towns,
And shiver off my sperm of wet dog-hair –

Night's claw, where cats couple among
The strict soldiering lupins. As afterthoughts,
My manners brush their teeth into the sink;
A cloud keeps my bed, the hot patch kept,
Warmth of armpits and incendiary struggles –
I return where my love gloats and swarms to sleep.

Imagine, if our naked bones
Broke up on these same stones, that freed stubble
Mouth jagged as smashed plastic –
Our nakedness breathes and shifts through warm
    holes,
Sighs from pricked gaps (the manners torn);
We know our natures and our flaws
Closer, from such uncharitable hunting . . .

I prise the blue-black feathers back. The **beak glows,**
Soft at the edges, like an urchin's valve –
Mouth. I know my own violence too.
I feel her gnawing, clinging, flesh-stubbed
Teeth in me, my remembrance of her mouth.
It is a killing but who dies?

I killed it slowly with a lump of flint.
Shot down and left to die, what soft thing jerks
Its pulped head, face, body, nerves
Beak-deep in the pasture mud? I watched
Those last sufferings leave her body too,
Twitching black and rook-supple before
I kicked my damaged violence into the wood.

Separation

Jetties suck, suck.
The broken and muddy water grips
Without purpose. The water has
Nowhere else to go, like ships.

Derricks could be of flesh
But seen through, X-rayed to the bone.
A gaunt skyline geometry,
Abstracts jerking out of human

Eyes a like jaggedness.
I imagine I see you borne
Bobbing on the brown water,
Your round eyes grey under the cold horn

Of the fog. And I touch
The river as if skin met skin,
A body identified
But crabbed, gelid, a frayed fraction,

A hermit grip rising out of the mud.
The parcel of sky, crammed, undelivered
Rains. All across the water
Tugs steam like burning dead.

In an instant the flayed river
Hisses up to the jetties
Crawling as if on legs. The ridge
Of that far bank disappears.

The river's itself. Your head
Bending down over the lettered keys
In your factory-loud office, feels
The waters surge back. You close your eyes.

Impression during an Interview

Both will lose face. The one
Nursing an idiocy
Unwinding his every word as if
The man he questioned was himself;
Gently, the gambit now a smile,
Wax to betray the mind's keyhole.

The other beginning to grope
For some brief abrading curse, which,
Circling, echoes back and back,
Through the multiple cancer that
Soars and lugs its steel-concrete
Dimension over both,
Like a broken and heavy wing,
Or a man's skull licked bare.

Clean Break

All winter the thudding sparrows came and went,
Despoiling our bread-crumb sill. And I lay in a
    sweat,
Watching them peck out, bit by bit,
The fabulous plenty of my heart.

Imagining their worst plight, I thought, my mind
    must break,
Imagining their budded claws, like scaffolding
Scrapping above the snow, and the bodies under the
    snow,
I lay, and could not dream;

And could not think. My brain refused such food,
But only lay and stared, until the walls, returning
Like an eavesdropping squad of surgeons, hemmed
    me in;
And I groped for signs of age, a first white hair . . .

Knowing, a man pays dearly who seldom thinks,
By having his thinking done for him;
Which is about as pleasant a trait as
Being cuckolded.

*

Now, in the warmth around me the rosebuds break
    alight;
My flesh glows dense; my arms, hooked like sickles
Encircle and clutch them; bind-weed, lupins, roots
Bitter as scammony, and the touch-me-not
Barbed squiggles of the centipedes' horned fingers.

All day the earth's on fire; I burn
With the damp rheumatisms of the loam,
A dense hydrangea-head among the tougher skulls,
Feeling the leather-jackets nip under the grass,

Under the winds that jump the furrows and tracks,
Winnowing slowly like a thresher at half-speed;

And lie, and gaze up at the sun where butter melts
Drop by drop on my hands, and stings, but heals.

Puddles

I cannot comfortably gaze at standing water.
Some focus seems to lie drowned there and waiting,
Eyeing upwards, among empty shells and bottle-caps,
At the waste features of the poring sky.
If clouds unbent at this moment and dazzled it grey
This deep puddle'd split, diminish, and with a gulp
Involve me, so my lancing fury'd break its bottom
Clean as a cupcrack – What would drain
Out, the weight of water, slimy tension of skin,
Might rise to collect me, much later,
And suddenly, when I'm feverish or weak.

At Rideau Falls

The tideless Ottawa is small
Beside the rivers of old Capitals;
Is logged by nylon-shirted men,
Match-makers. At Rideau Falls
I watch, drunk, the thrust of a barge
Bruising my ribs with each lurch, coils
Of surf stampeding up the night.
I will not come back. My time
Outlingers cities; my warm children
Rest surly in my head. They will own
This germ of me that failed to grow.
They will pick stark fables from my bones.

The Crèche

The crèche of faces, like wintering crocuses, lay mute under their cauls of white wool. I stood at the extreme end of the room, facing the wide fissured mirror, and tried to identify one child that had its fingers twisted to a hard ball in the rough smock of homespun the nuns had sewn him into.

This one, I knew, was not pitted and scarred like the others, but would have slept in a silksoft crib and blue initialled sheets in the now heavily shelled château. The lamps, looking like nuns' wimples, hung over the stark lines of cots, stiff and crisp, starched cotton such as I'd dreamed of, feeling the lice nip deep in my thick socks, touching tenderly the crescent weal on my belly where the rat had clung scrabbling with its claws.

His face, I sensed, would be free of scars and sores, something perhaps crying a little, softly, to itself, that its guardians could not get at now to retrieve. In the glaring silence of the fusty ward I could still, though barely, hear the seventy-fives, and the bigger guns, one-five-fives and naval guns, and the heavy soft flocculent heave of the mortar-bursts. Looking more intently now, I realized there wasn't time, that soon the tanks, the armoured cars, and the Taubes would be circling the village, and an inky smoke would blot up all daylight at the wire-barred windows of the room, making further searches impractical.

So I shouted out my own name; and the long cot lines froze suddenly still, as if the first mortar shell had just now snapped the roof. But nothing moved or spoke, or cried even, and I saw that the nuns had gone away taking their clay jars and crucifixes with them, out of the village. The face I was searching for lay there, among the others, undiscoverable; and sleeping, I imagined, but with its pink shocked mouth open wide on a high silent wailing that followed me, like the sharp tuning-forks of bullets striking the wires, as I stumbled out into the soft April mud, haunted and nameless, as before, belonging nowhere.

I Think I am Becoming Myself

This is life at the marrow,
No-telling and secretive. In this quiet month
All appearance has been merely figurative;
Whatever I touch might prove the prime mover.

Patience is a tact due to time –
Old fashioned and ungrateful. So my hands
Miss your plain body, every shape of limb
Grows huge exaggerated as eucalyptus'
Smooth wind-sucking dormant tension of sap.

If the tree should wilt and close up,
Under the dream and the dream's fantasy
And under that, in a detritus quicksand of blind
Thick wanting –
What? There life is cold, adequate,
The order bland, the senses blunt as dead tools.

No, this is life at the core, time single.
Beyond this is just a waiting on dates: time
Told by clocks is not time of blood.
Bare objects attend and listen –
Our reunion will be slow and cautious and final.

Index of First Lines